the COL

GW00631123

Ash

SAGE
PRESS

Published in 2001

SAGE PRESS,
PO Box Nº 1, Rye, East Sussex TN36 6HN.
e.mail: sagepress.bm@btinternet.com   www.sagepress.co.uk
© Sage Press 2001

Set in Palatine italic 9 on 11 point leading.
Display in Palatino Light Italic 48 point.

*Design and Illustrations*
Chris Monk of Yellowduck Design & Illustration.

*Research & Text*
Cindy Stevens

*Series Editor and Publisher*
Mrs Bobby Meyer

Printed by M & W Morgan Printers, Hastings

ISBN: 0 - 9531644 – 7 – 0

# Ash

*'The Venus of the forest'…'The husbandman's tree' …*

*The ash is the second most important indigenous tree in Britain and has been well established here since about 6,000 BC. It is very distinctive in appearance, with its stark winter outline, its feathery summer foliage and its bunches of seed pods or 'keys'. It has important connections with mythology and folklore and many practical uses, although it is less valued now than formerly.*

*The seventeenth century diarist John Evelyn, said: 'so useful and profitable is this tree, next to Oak, that every prudent Lord of a Manor should employ one acre of ground with Ash to every other 20 acres of land, since in as many years it would be worth more than the land itself.'*

*A century later, the writer and artist, William Gilpin, was also praising the tree: 'Nothing can have a better effect than an old ash, hanging from the corner of a wood and bringing off the heaviness of the other foliage, with its loose pendant branches.'*

## Ash in mythology

Ash has a
particularly important
place in the Teutonic mythology
of Northern Europe. In
Scandinavia it was known
as Yggdrasil, *the tree representing the cosmos and
providing a bridge for the gods between the heavenly and
earthly spheres. The three Fates – Past, Present and Future
– sat at its feet and watered it from the Sacred Well, fed
in turn by the Sacred Fountain of Destiny. Its branches
held the heavens, its trunk the middle earth and its roots
the underworld. The gods would meet, under the
leadership of Odin, to take counsel in its shade.*

*According to the legend a golden cock watched from
the topmost branches to warn the gods if their old
enemies, the Giants, were approaching. In German
mythology, however, the bird was an eagle and there
was a squirrel running up and down the tree to
warn those waiting below.*

*Ash also features in the creation myth. It was the
Norse god Odin, with his brothers, who created the
first man, Ask, from an ash tree. The first woman,
Embla, was created from another tree,
possibly an elm or, in some versions, a vine.*

Through the centuries ash has often been considered a protector. The Ancient Greeks valued it highly and made it sacred to Poseidon, the god of the sea. Seafarers believed that a cross made from ash wood protected them from drowning. More recently, in other parts of Europe, it was seen as a defence against evil and spells. Its leaves and wood were kept in the house, and herdsmen carried ash sticks to protect their cattle against witchcraft.

Ash was used for divination and had associations with love; hence its name 'Venus of the forest'. In some parts of Britain, leaves with an even number of divisions on each side were considered to be a sign of good fortune and were used by young girls hoping for a husband.

A girl would
pick such a leaf
while reciting :
'Even, even ash
'I pluck thee off the tree
'The first young man that I do meet
'My lover shall he be.'

She would then keep the leaf in her left shoe until she met her man!

More locally, in Sussex, the ash was seen as a tree of magic and mystery. Richard Mabey in Flora Britannica, quotes a description of children being taught never to harm it and 'never to pass an ash-tree without wishing it 'good-day'…'. The tradition still holds for Desirée Merican of Shoreham-by-Sea, who says: "I still hold the ash as a tree to be respected, and find myself furtively dipping and bidding whenever I pass one."

There are other British folk traditions associated with ash. The ashen faggot is the Devon and Somerset version of the yule log. A thick faggot of green ash-sticks tied with ash or hazel thongs, or brambles, would be brought indoors with great ceremony on Christmas Eve. It was intended to burn for the entire twelve days of Christmas and so would be very thick and as wide as the hearth would allow. Sometimes it was so heavy that it had to be held in place by chains.

In 1952, the ashen faggot burnt at the New Inn in Northleigh, Devon weighed one hundredweight (about 50 kg). It was five foot (1.5 m)

long, eighteen inches (45 cm) thick and bound with five bands of hazel.
The bands binding the faggot played an important part in the ritual.
As each band burned through and so burst, there would be toasts
and cider-drinking. Young people would each choose a band to see
who would marry first: the earlier the band burst, the sooner
marriage would come.

Although the faggot was usually bound with only four or five bands,
nine or more were not unknown and provided a good excuse for
drinking. For the 1836 celebrations at Torwood Manor in Devon, the
faggot was drawn in by a team of four oxen. With the bursting of each
band, a fresh gallon of cider was provided for all present.

Domestic hearths became smaller, but nonetheless the tradition
continued with miniature faggots being burned in private homes.
In neighbouring Somerset, the traditional date for burning the faggot
was sometimes St Catherine's Day (24 November).

Although the ash tree has nothing to do with Ash Wednesday, Mabey found memories of a children's ritual in Kent on that day. Each child would go to school carrying an ash twig with at least one black bud on it. Failure to do so would result in having one's feet stamped on. The position was reversed after midday, when those who had forgotten to get rid of their twigs would have their feet stamped on by those who had done so. Mabey offers no explanation for this bizarre ritual.

Another popular children's game in some areas was 'mud yacks', where ash poles were used to propel balls of mud, sometimes over considerable distances. The pole would be bent back like a bow and the mud ball flicked as high and as far as possible.

Many other traditions are concerned with the weather or with the medicinal properties of ash.

# The uses of Ash

## Medicinal

There have been many medicinal uses for ash in the past, some of which are straightforward herbal ones while others belong more to the realm of folklore.

Writing in the eighteenth century, Gilbert White describes a traditional cure for rickets which was practiced in the village of Selborne. Several pollarded ash trees were split and wedged open. On three consecutive mornings, children suffering from rickets or similar ailments would be passed naked through the gaps. The wedges were then removed and the split 'plastered with loam and carefully swathed up. If the parts coalesced and soldered together… the party was cured.'

In other parts of the country, simply passing a child through a split ash tree was thought to cure rupture. This same ritual was used to cure many other ailments in both children and adults.

An even more bizarre cure involved a shrew to cure cramp and lameness, chiefly in cattle but also in humans. The little animal (thought to be the cause of the illness, for reasons which are now unclear) would be trapped inside a hole made in an ash branch.

There was a widespread belief, dating at least from the first century physician Dioscorides, that the juice of the leaves was an antidote to snake-bite: 'The juice of the leaves or the leaves themselves are of so greate virtue against serpents that they dare not so much as touch the morning and evening shadows of the tree, but shun them afar off' according to Pliny. The sixteenth century herbalist John Gerard, when quoting this, recommended both applying the leaves directly to the stings and drinking the juice in wine. However, Nicholas Culpeper, some fifty years later, rejected the idea that there was any truth in this theory.

The wood itself was even thought to cure warts! In some places there was a tradition of pricking each wart with a pin which was then placed in an ash tree while this charm was repeated :

'Ashen tree, ashen tree,
'Pray take these warts of me.'

Such was the traditional conviction that the tree could heal that nail clippings or locks of hair would be attached to the trunk in an attempt to cure a wide variety of ailments, from ringworm and whooping cough to earache and impotence.

In Scotland, it is said that midwives practised the dubious tradition of putting one end of a fresh ash stick in the fire and collecting the sap oozing from the other end to give the new-born baby as its first food.

St Hildegard of Bingen and many later herbalists recommended the use of ash in cases of gout, which is perhaps the reason for it sometimes being known as 'the gout tree'.

There are indeed many remedies attributed to the different parts of this wonderful tree. Culpeper recommended taking an extract of the leaves soaked in water, before breakfast, to combat both dropsy and obesity. The young leaves and green seeds are still used today for their diuretic and laxative properties. An infusion of the leaves taken every four weeks was thought to act as a general health tonic, even prolonging life.

Culpeper also found uses for various parts of the tree in cases of jaundice, and digestive and scalp problems. Today many treatments still hold. Modern herbalists, for instance, use the bark of young trees as a digestive tonic, and have found ash is effective in treating diarrhoea, bleeding and fever: interestingly Messegué called it the quinine of Europe.

For the more adventurous, boiling the ash 'keys' in water is thought by some to produce a drink with aphrodisiacal properties!

# Timber

Because of the importance of its wood, for which there are so many practical and medicinal uses, ash was once widely coppiced. In its natural state, the tree rarely lives for more than 200 years but a tree coppiced every ten years can go on almost indefinitely. There is a fine such coppiced specimen in Bradfield Woods, Suffolk, which is estimated to be over 1000 years old and has a diameter of nearly six metres.

Throughout the British Isles there are many traces of ash coppicing having been practised in woodlands over the centuries, as well as evidence of ancient pollarding in hedgerows.

Further afield it is known that ash timber was greatly valued by the Ancient Egyptians who imported it, together with cypress, cedar and box, from Syria.

The wood has a pale-pinkish tinge when first cut, drying to white. It dries very well, is good for sawing and machine-turning, cleaves easily and is particularly suitable for steam-bending. As the most elastic of British woods, it was of particular value where the springiness of its shock-absorbing qualities were required for wheel-making, and its decline in

*importance in recent times may reflect the use of alternative materials for these purposes.*

*Ash is not generally used for decorative purposes since it has a very strong, wrinkled grain, although some consider it to be an attractive furniture wood. It needs to be treated if it is to come into direct contact with the ground. The name 'ash' comes from the Anglo-Saxon aesc, and it was indeed widely used for making spears in the past. Arrows and, later, pikeshafts were frequently made of ash.*

*In more recent times its uses were many. Ash was much in demand for the frames of carriages and wagons because it was so tough yet could be pressed into shape after boiling or steaming. Even the bodywork of early cars and aircraft were often made of ash, while the chassis of Morgan cars are still made in this way, Morgan having their own woodland for the purpose.*

*Under iron tyres the wheel-rims of carts and carriages were almost invariably of ash, because it is such a good shock-absorber; they were made up of alternating porous spring wood and dense summer wood. Sledges are often made of ash for the same reasons.*

*It is a versatile wood, of value also in very heavy work, such as early railway sleepers and rails, and the heavy framing of windmills. The straight growth which*

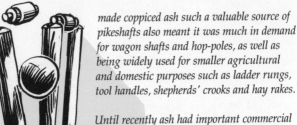

made coppiced ash such a valuable source of pikeshafts also meant it was much in demand for wagon shafts and hop-poles, as well as being widely used for smaller agricultural and domestic purposes such as ladder rungs, tool handles, shepherds' crooks and hay rakes.

Until recently ash had important commercial use for many items of sports equipment. The toughest specimens would be selected from special plantations grown by the manufacturers and used for cricket stumps, hockey stick heads, skis, polo sticks, fishing rods, billiard cues and parts of tennis racquets.

Walking sticks or 'ashplants' are made from young trees – two to three years of age - heated in damp sand and bent in a curved vice. An alternative method in southern England was to grow the ash specifically for the purpose: one to two year old seedlings would be planted at an angle with the end nipped off so that the tree would have to grow from a side-shoot. This then became the shaft while the original stem was the handle. This process is still carried out today on a limited scale.

Other uses include frames for traditional crab and lobster pots in Northumberland and bent work in furniture and boats. The great elasticity of the wood made it ideal for catapults and children would seek out wood with a natural fork for this very purpose.

Ash makes excellent fuel charcoal, although not suitable for gunpowder or artists' charcoal. It should be added that it is illegal to use sound trees for the purpose, and has been so since 1585. It is also very good for logs, as it burns without smoke when dry and does not need to be seasoned:

'Burn ash-wood green,
Tis fit for a queen.'

An anonymous rhyme, Logs to Burn, after listing various types of wood, concludes:

'But ash logs, all smooth and grey,
'Burn them green or old;
'Buy up all that comes your way,
'They're worth their weight in gold.'

The catalogue of uses for this fascinating tree appears almost endless: even the astringent bark played a role, namely in the fishing industry as a tanning agent for the nets.

Occasionally, like other important trees, the ash has been used as a boundary marker. In medieval times we know there was one such marker ash growing between the parishes of East Chiltington and St John Without near Lewes in Sussex and whose probable remains are still visible today.

## Ash as food

Young ash shoots can be picked and boiled like asparagus tips. The keys are tasty when pickled with salt and vinegar for use in sauces and salads. John Evelyn said "Ashen keys have the virtue of capers"

## Ash in literature

Ash features frequently in writings about rural life. In his poem Remembrances, John Clare describes how :
'We sought the hollow ash that was shelter from the rain.'

And the Dorset dialect poet William Barnes refers to the ash in Winter A-Comen:
'Your walks in the ash-tree droves be cwold…'.

In Trees, Walter de la Mare wrote
'Of all the trees in England,
Her sweet three corners in,
Only the Ash, the bonnie Ash
Burns fierce while it is green'.

*Art*

*Ash was the favourite tree of John Constable and there are many examples in his paintings. His biographer described the 'ecstasy of delight' with which he would admire a tree. 'All who are acquainted with his pictures cannot fail to have observed how frequently (an ash tree) is introduced as a near object, and how beautifully its distinguishing particularities are marked.' Towering ash trees stand at the entrance to 'The Cornfield', for example, while 'A Study of Ash and Other Trees' shows the delicacy of their foliage.*

*Once, when giving a lecture at Hampstead, Constable used as illustration a 'tall and elegant ash' which he had drawn nearby, saying: 'Many of my Hampstead friends may remember this young lady at the entrance to the village. Her fate was distressing, for it is scarcely too much to say that she died of a broken heart… A wretched board (was) nailed to her side…'.*

*The tree seems to have felt the disgrace and died, after which it was unfeelingly 'cut down to a stump, just high enought to hold the board.'*

## Country lore

Ash has its special place in weather prediction. Most often, traditional rhymes suggest that the summer will be wet if the ash is in leaf before the oak, but it seems that things are different in Surrey:

'If the oak comes out before the ash.
'Twill be a year of mix and splash.
'If the ash comes out before the oak,
'Twill be a year of fire and smoke.'
In fact, ash is usually very late to leaf whether the season is wet or dry.

## Place names

Ash has given its name to many places. Askrigg, in North Yorkshire, means ash ridge. Ashurst, in Sussex and also in Hampshire, means ash wood. There are Ashtons and Ashbys, a Downash, a Nash, an Ashwick, an Askham, an Ashlington and many others. Aspatria, in Cumbria, means Patrick's ash.

Ash is so widespread in Britain, growing wild right up to the Outer Hebrides and the far north of Scotland, that it is not surprising that so many places bear its name.

## Ash in the landscape

The tall, shapely, delicately leaved tree beloved of Constable is never long-lived but can give pleasure for a century or more. 'Its chief beauty consists in the lightness of its whole appearance', says Gilpin. Ash woods let in much light and so are usually full of flowers, especially in spring when carpeted with snowdrops, wood anemones and bluebells.

Ash coppices are quite different, since the regular cutting gives great longevity and the trees may 'become the immemorial, gnarled and mossy coppice stools of ancient woodlands', says Owen Johnson. These stools may be very large and are usually gnarled, with knobs of scar tissue showing where they have survived years of attack by livestock.

Ash seeds profusely and has come to be considered as a 'weed tree' by some foresters now that its timber is less in demand. One of its common names is in fact Hampshire weed. *In* The Well Tempered Garden, *Christopher Lloyd describes weeding 807 ash seedlings out of a flower bed containing only 24 rose bushes.*

Ash can grow in very poor ground and is found on limestone pavement above the Yorkshire Dales where even the sheep cannot reach. For commercial purposes, it is best planted on rich soil where it can grow quickly and produce tougher wood.

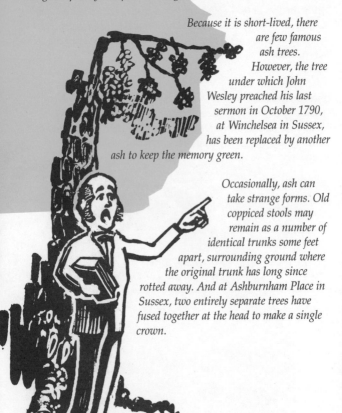

Because it is short-lived, there are few famous ash trees. However, the tree under which John Wesley preached his last sermon in October 1790, at Winchelsea in Sussex, has been replaced by another ash to keep the memory green.

Occasionally, ash can take strange forms. Old coppiced stools may remain as a number of identical trunks some feet apart, surrounding ground where the original trunk has long since rotted away. And at Ashburnham Place in Sussex, two entirely separate trees have fused together at the head to make a single crown.

*Ash to Christopher Lloyd is '....a tree of contrasts if ever there was one; so uncompromisingly stark in its winter outline...but diaphanous and feathery in summer, never casting a deep, glum shade...'*

'Of all the trees that grow so fair,
'Old England to adorn,
'Greater are none beneath the sun
'Than Oak, and Ash, and Thorn'
(Kipling, A Tree Song)

**Common name:** *Ash*

**Botanical name:**
*Fraxinus excelsior*

**Family:** *Oleaceae*

**Growth:** *Resists exposure well; self-seeds freely. Average natural lifespan 200 years but can live much longer if coppiced.*

**Flowers:** *Insignificant, with no sepals or petals, usually appearing at the same time as the leaves. May be male, female or bisexual, sometimes all on the same tree. Grows in clusters hanging from short stalks.*

**Bark:** *Pale grey with a ribbed appearance.*

**Size:** *height 25-35 metres (although can reach 45 metres), girth rarely more than six metres.*

*Bud, and above, in flower*

*Fruit:*
Ash 'keys'.
Conspicuous
bunches of
winged seed
pods, each
containing
one seed.
May remain
on the tree
well into the winter. Sometimes known as
'spinners' because of the way they travel on the wind.

*Leaves:* Deciduous, very late to
appear and quite early to fall.
May be as much as 25 cm long,
composed of 7-15 pairs and a single
terminal leaflet. Each leaflet is oval,
pointed and serrated. Very
distinctive black buds in winter.

In the same series
*Box*
*Cedar of Lebanon*
*Hawthorn*
*Holly*
*Monkey Puzzle*
*Oak*
*Yew*


To be published soon
*Beech*
*Birch*
*Catalpa*
*Elm*
*Hornbeam*
*Mulberry*
*Scots Pine*
*Willow*


If you enjoyed this title and would like
to buy any of the above titles
or require further information
please contact


**SAGE PRESS**
PO Box N° 1, Rye, East Sussex TN31 6HN.
e-mail: sagepress.bm@btinternet.com
Website: sagepress.co.uk